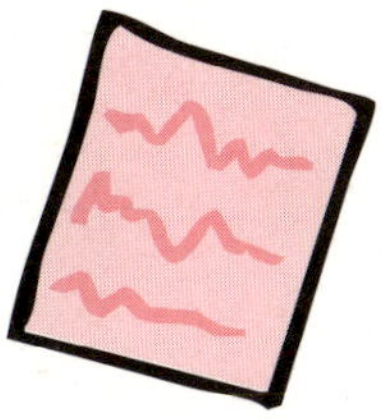
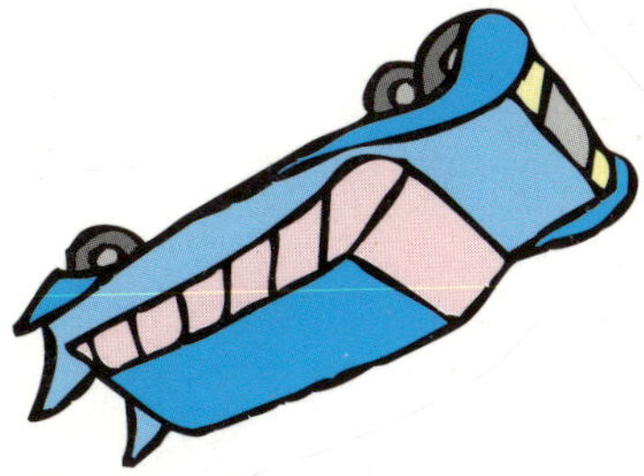
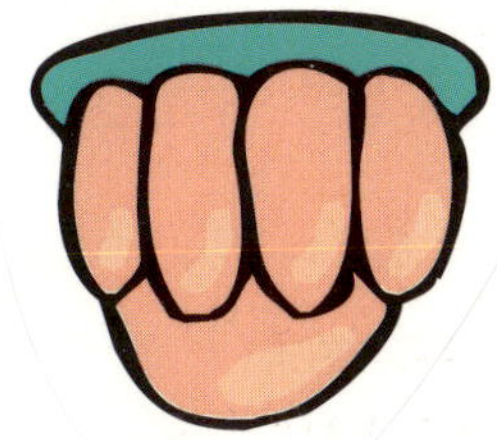

MONSTER MATHS

Letts

Christabell

HOBBIES Playing games on her laptop computer
SKILL Technology whizz
FAVOURITE COLOURS Pink and red
LIVES Smile Street with Ezzo, Waldo and Whiffy

Ezzo

HOBBIES Kung fu
STRENGTH Martial Arts expert
BEST MOVE Karate kick
FAVOURITE FILMS Monster action films

Waldo

FAVOURITE FOOD Dog biscuits
HOBBIES Biting squeaky toys
STRANGE FACT Can change shape
OWNER Ezzo

Whiffy

FAVOURITE FOOD Cakes with lots of icing
HOBBIES Playing, dancing
STRANGE FACT Turns to invisible vapour when afraid and makes a terrible smell

P (a.k.a. Princess)

HOBBIES Scheming to take over Monster City
STRENGTH Deadly scream that knocks everybody out
LIKES Sparkly things, parties

Edgar

HOBBIES Making machines to take over Monster City
SKILL Brilliant scientist
BEST INVENTION Gripping bow tie
BEST FRIEND P

Flob

HOBBIES Monster TV
BEST FRIEND P won't let him have friends, because she doesn't want any
LIKES Eating yummy food until his tummy is about to pop

One day, everybody in Monster City got an invitation written on shiny, pink paper. It said, "Come to a fancy dress ball at the old palace. There will be a big surprise. From P."

"What is a ball?" Whiffy asked.

"It is a very big party with lots of dancing and food," Christabell explained.

"That sounds good. I am a great dancer," Whiffy replied excitedly. "I wonder what the surprise will be?"

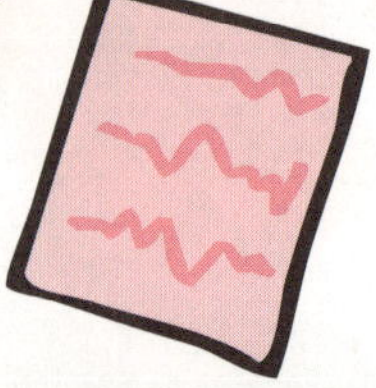

Put your invitation on the right spot at the front of the book, so you can go to the ball too!

1 Counting to 100

If every monster in Monster City got an invitation to the ball, that would be a lot of monsters! We would have to be able to count to at least 100 to see how many guests were invited. Practise by reading out loud all of the numbers in Christabell's special number grid.

1	2	3	4	5	6	7	8	9	10
11	12	13	14	15	16	17	18	19	20
21	22	23	24	25	26	27	28	29	30
31	32	33	34	35	36	37	38	39	40
41	42	43	44	45	46	47	48	49	50
51	52	53	54	55	56	57	58	59	60
61	62	63	64	65	66	67	68	69	70
71	72	73	74	75	76	77	78	79	80
81	82	83	84	85	86	87	88	89	90
91	92	93	94	95	96	97	98	99	100

2 Tens and units

Christabell says there will be lots of delicious food at the ball. Using tens and units will help you to add up the number of cakes on a big plate. This big plate has 16 cakes on it.

10 + 6 = 16

tens units

Use Christabell's grid to help you write in the missing numbers in these number chains.

1 10 ___ 12 13 ___ 15 ___ 17 18 ___

2 80 81 82 83 ___ ___ 86 ___ 88

3 ___ 41 42 ___ ___ 45 46 ___ 48 49

4 71 ___ 73 ___ ___ 76 ___ 78 ___ 80

5 34 ___ 36 37 ___ ___ 40 ___ 42 43

6 85 ___ ___ 88 89 ___ 91 92 ___ ___

7 ___ 48 49 ___ 51 ___ ___ 54 ___ 56

8 69 ___ ___ 72 ___ 74 75 ___ 77 ___

9 ___ ___ 93 94 95 ___ 97 98 ___ ___

10 ___ ___ 55 56 ___ ___ 59 ___ 61 62

See if you can separate these numbers into tens and units or add them together to make a new number. Think of big plates of cakes if it helps!

1 ___ + ___ = 18

2 ___ + ___ = 24

3 ___ + ___ = 59

4 90 + 8 = ___

5 60 + 5 = ___

6 ___ + ___ = 73

7 ___ + ___ = 82

8 30 + 4 = ___

9 40 + 6 = ___

10 ___ + ___ = 54

The day before the ball Ezzo made himself a pirate costume with a wooden sword. Christabell made herself a fairy costume with a gold wand. Even Waldo had a costume. Ezzo made him a collar shaped like a flower.

Whiffy made the best costume. He stuck feathers all over an old t-shirt and made a beak out of paper.

"Cheep, cheep! I am a bird!" he cried and flapped his arms. "I am going to make up a bird dance to do at the ball."

You can't dance without music! Take your tambourine so you can play a tune for Whiffy.

3 Adding sets

Here is a set of wooden swords and a set of golden wands, just like the ones Ezzo and Christabell made for their costumes. Count the set of swords and the set of wands. Then add them up to see how many there are altogether.

$$9 + 12 = 21$$

4 Taking away sets

Every time Whiffy took more feathers out of the set in the pillow, the set of feathers in the pillow got smaller and smaller.

If there was a set of 10 feathers in the pillow and Whiffy used a set of 4 for his costume, there would be 6 feathers left in the set in the pillow.

$$10 - 4 = 6$$

Write down how many swords and how many wands there are in each set. Then add them together.

1 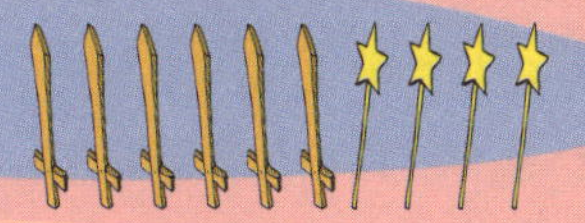 □ + □ = □

2  □ + □ = □

3 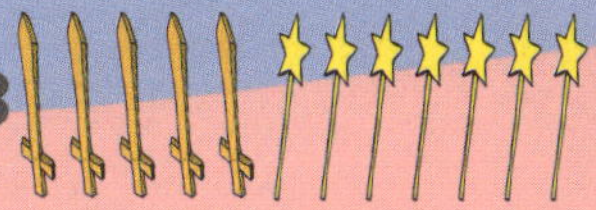 □ + □ = □

4  □ + □ = □

5 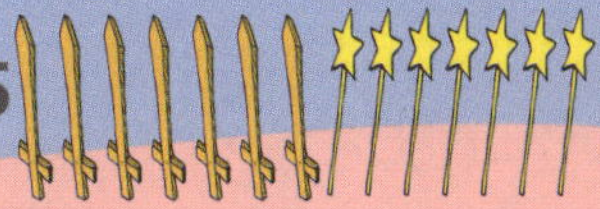 □ + □ = □

6  □ + □ = □

7 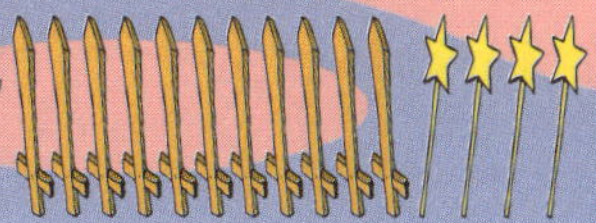 □ + □ = □

8 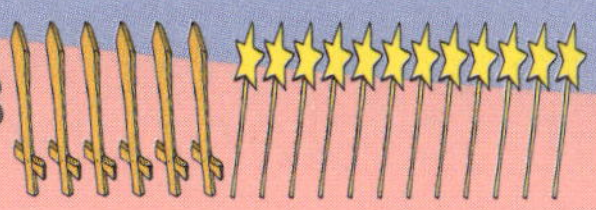 □ + □ = □

9  □ + □ = □

10  □ + □ = □

Here are some piles of feathers. Write down how many will be left in the set, when some have been used for Whiffy's bird costume.

1 

□ – □ = □

2 

□ – □ = □

3 

□ – □ = □

4 

□ – □ = □

5 

□ – □ = □

6 

□ – □ = □

7 

□ – □ = □

8 

□ – □ = □

9 

□ – □ = □

10 

□ – □ = □

Whiffy was so excited he went to bed in his costume. But the feathers tickled him and made him giggle. In the end, he had to take his costume off.

When Whiffy went to sleep he dreamt about being at the ball. In his dream he was dancing with a beautiful princess. She told him he had won a prize for dancing. “Here it is,” she said, giving him a gold crown and a plate of cakes with chocolate icing on top.

Monsters love yummy cakes! Put some in the right place on your party list.

5 Missing numbers

At the moment, Whiffy is happy and excited about the ball. But when he's frightened, he becomes invisible. Some of the numbers in these sums are invisible, too. What clues are there to help you find them?

$$12 + \_ = 18 \qquad 18 - \_ = 6$$

The clue is that both sums have the number 18 in them, even though it's in a different place.

$$12 + 6 = 18 \qquad 18 - 12 = 6$$

The same three numbers are used in both sums.

6 Adding and taking away tens

Christabell is so excited about the ball, she can't sleep. So she adds up and takes away tens in her head, which soon makes her as dreamy as Whiffy!

Adding tens is just like adding units. See if you can spot the pattern.

$$5 + 4 = 9$$
$$50 + 40 = 90$$

Use the clues in these sets of sums to write in the invisible numbers.

1 10 + __ = 14   14 − __ = 4

2 9 + __ = 14   14 − __ = 5

3 16 + __ = 18   18 − __ = 2

4 12 + __ = 19   19 − __ = 7

5 __ + 12 = 17   17 − 5 = __

6 __ + 15 = 22   22 − __ = 7

7 9 + 8 = __   17 − 8 = __

8 17 + __ = 22   __ − 17 = 5

9 __ + 11 = 31   31 − 20 = __

10 __ + 15 = 29   29 − __ = 14

Write down the answers to these sums, but try not fall asleep like Whiffy and Christabell!

1 3 + 5 = __
30 + 50 = __

2 6 + 4 = __
60 + 40 = __

3 3 + 3 = __
30 + 30 = __

4 4 + 2 = __
40 + 20 = __

5 6 + 7 = __
60 + 70 = __

6 2 + 9 = __
20 + 90 = __

7 8 + 5 = __
80 + 50 = __

8 7 + 10 = __
70 + 100 = __

9 12 + 4 = __
120 + 40 = __

10 16 + 9 = __
160 + 90 = __

When Whiffy woke up the next morning, he simply couldn't wait to find out more about the ball. Without eating breakfast, he headed off to the palace, crept inside and hid behind a sofa. But he forgot that he was always very smelly.

P, Edgar and Flob came into the room carrying balloons for the party.

"It is a bit smelly in here," P sniffed as she looked around. "Who cares! Tell us about the party," Flob begged P.

P likes balloons, so you'd better take some of those to the ball too!

7 Adding money

Whiffy had to walk past a bakery on the way to the palace. But he was far too excited to stop and eat anything. He had 35p in his pocket – enough to buy a crusty roll (15p) and currant bun (20p).

15p + 20p = 35p

8 Taking away money

Whiffy's too excited to think about his breakfast. So let's buy it for him. If we had 80p, and we bought a sausage sandwich for 60p, we would be left with 20p. So we could buy a currant bun with the change!

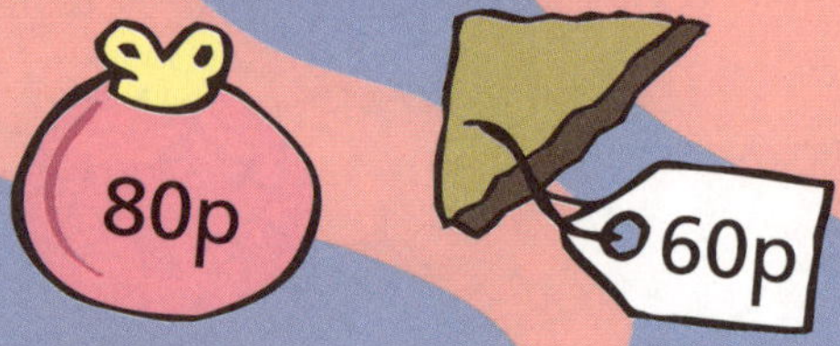

80p – 60p = 20p

Add up how much it would cost to buy these things at the bakery. Then write the amounts in the spaces.

1. 5p + 12p = ☐p
2. 22p + 7p = ☐p
3. 50p + 16p = ☐p
4. 11p + 23p = ☐p
5. 61p + 9p = ☐p
6. 72p + 20p = ☐p
7. 16p + 43p = ☐p
8. 24p + 61p = ☐p
9. 8p + 88p = ☐p
10. 43p + 46p = ☐p

Write down how much money you would have left after buying Whiffy's breakfast.

1. 40p – 20p = ☐p
2. 75p – 25p = ☐p
3. 20p – 16p = ☐p
4. 95p – 55p = ☐p
5. 24p – 12p = ☐p
6. 68p – 48p = ☐p
7. 73p – 41p = ☐p
8. 49p – 37p = ☐p
9. 96p – 59p = ☐p
10. £1.00 – 42p = ☐p

Whiffy felt excited. Would the surprise be a giant chocolate cake or a fireworks show? Or would it be a prize for the best dancer at the ball? He secretly hoped it would be!

"When all the guests have arrived, I shall stand up to make a speech," P began. "Then I will give them their surprise."

Whiffy listened hard, and so did Flob and Edgar, who were still holding their balloons. "I will open my mouth and scream," cried P, as she cackled like a witch.

Whiffy wants a giant chocolate cake, so add one to your party list.

9 Shapes

Whiffy had seen lots of different balloon shapes at other monster parties. But he had never seen the shapes that Edgar and Flob were carrying!

10 Measuring

How big would Whiffy's dream chocolate cake be? 1cm high? Or 3cm high? Or even 5cm high?

Perhaps his dream chocolate cake is even higher than that!

Write down the shape of each balloon, then how many sides it has.

1  A ____________ has ☐ sides.

2  A ____________ has ☐ sides.

3 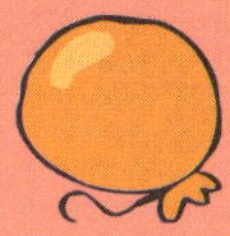 A ____________ has ☐ sides.

4  A ____________ has ☐ sides.

5  A ____________ has ☐ sides.

6  A ____________ has ☐ sides.

7  A ____________ has ☐ sides.

8  A ____________ has ☐ sides.

9  A ____________ has ☐ sides.

10  A ____________ has ☐ sides.

Use the ruler to help you draw the chocolate cakes to the right size. Then write down the answers to the questions.

1 Draw a cake 2cm high.

2 Draw a cake 5cm high.

3 Draw a cake 1cm high.

4 Draw a cake 4cm high.

5 Is cake 3 bigger than cake 1? ____

6 Is cake 4 bigger than cake 1? ____

7 Is cake 2 smaller than cake 4? ____

8 Is cake 1 smaller than cake 4? ____

9 Is cake 4 bigger than cake 3? ____

10 Is cake 3 bigger than cake 2? ____

"My scream will be loud enough to knock out all the party guests," P remarked. "I can do it perfectly as long as nobody makes me laugh. Then, when everyone wakes up, I will threaten to scream again unless I'm made Queen of Monster City."

P was so pleased with her plan that she did a dance, then popped a balloon with her fingernail. The bang made Whiffy jump and he let out a gasp.

"What was that?" P snapped.

P is planning an evil plot! You had better take her a present to make her happy. How about a sparkling crown?

11 Groups of 2 and 3

Whiffy imagines P's guests arriving in groups of 2 or 3, then entering the big room where the ball will take place.

He counts up lots of groups of 2 monsters.

$$2 + 2 + 2 + 2 = 8$$

Then he counts up lots of groups of 3 monsters.

$$3 + 3 + 3 = 9$$

12 Groups of 4 and 5

Whiffy jumped when P popped the balloon. He decided to count how many groups of balloons were left for the party.

$$4 + 4 + 4 = 12$$

Just these three groups of four balloons, making tweleve balloons not popped by P.

Add up these groups of 2 and 3 to work out the total number.

1. 2+2+2=□
2. 3+3+3+3=□
3. □+□+□+□+□=□
4. □+□+□=□
5. □+□+□+□+□+□=□
6. □+□+□+□+□+□+□+□=□
7. □+□+□+□+□+□=□
8. □+□=□
9. □+□+□+□+□+□+□=□
10. □+□+□+□+□=□

Add together these sets of balloons and write down the answers. Some have 4 in a set and some have 5.

1. 4+4+4+4+4+4=□
2. 5+5+5=□
3. □+□+□+□=□
4. □+□+□+□+□+□+□=□
5. □+□+□+□+□=□
6. □+□+□+□+□+□+□+□=□
7. □+□+□+□+□+□=□
8. □+□+□+□=□
9. □+□+□+□+□=□
10. □+□+□+□+□+□+□+□+□=□

P moved towards the sofa, looking evil. Whiffy suddenly felt scared and his knees knocked together. His smell got much worse. When Whiffy gets very smelly, his body turns into smelly vapours and he becomes invisible! So P didn't see him.

"Pooh!" said Flob. "Did you make that smell, Edgar?"

"No! I thought it was you! It's disgusting!" Edgar cried.

"Well, it wasn't me," P protested.

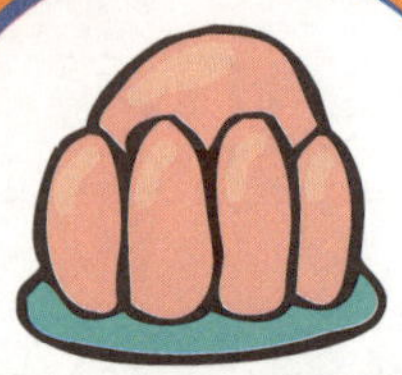

Poor Whiffy turns to vapours when he gets scared. His knees becomes like pink jelly! Take your jelly to the party.

13 2 times table

P was so pleased with her plan, that she sang a little song ...

"2, 4, 6, 8! Who do we appreciate? Me! Soon to be Queen of Monster City!"

Christabell would know that 2, 4, 6, 8 is the beginning of the 2 times table, because she is very good at maths. Say your 2 times table out loud to practise it.

$1 \times 2 = 2$	$6 \times 2 = 12$
$2 \times 2 = 4$	$7 \times 2 = 14$
$3 \times 2 = 6$	$8 \times 2 = 16$
$4 \times 2 = 8$	$9 \times 2 = 18$
$5 \times 2 = 10$	$10 \times 2 = 20$

14 3 times table

Whiffy is so scared, he is getting smellier and smellier! One way he could calm down and take his mind of scary matters, would be to practise his 3 times table! You could practise it, too.

$1 \times 3 = 3$	$6 \times 3 = 18$
$2 \times 3 = 6$	$7 \times 3 = 21$
$3 \times 3 = 9$	$8 \times 3 = 24$
$4 \times 3 = 12$	$9 \times 3 = 27$
$5 \times 3 = 15$	$10 \times 3 = 30$

Write in the missing numbers from these sums using your 2 times table.

1	3	×	2	=	
2	7	×	2	=	
3	6	×		=	12
4		×	2	=	4
5		×	2	=	20
6	8	×	2	=	
7		×	2	=	10
8		×	2	=	14
9		×	2	=	8
10	9	×	2	=	

Now see if you can fill in the missing numbers from these sums.

1	3	×	3	=	
2	6	×	3	=	
3	7	×		=	21
4	9	×	3	=	
5		×	3	=	15
6	8	×	3	=	
7	4	×	3	=	
8		×	3	=	6
9		×	3	=	30
10	7	×	3	=	

While P, Flob and Edgar argued, Whiffy crept away from the sofa and hurried all the way back to Smile Street.

"P is going to scream until we make her Queen of Monster City, unless we can find a way to make her laugh at the party," he told his friends sadly. Christabell opened her handbag and switched on the laptop computer hidden inside it. She found some jokes and started reading them out loud. But although everyone smiled, they did not laugh.

Could you make the Smile Street gang laugh? How about a clown nose and glasses for your costume?

15 10 times table

P's scream is 10 times noisier than any other scream you can imagine. No wonder the friendly monsters want to find a way to make her laugh!

The 10 times table is easy to learn. You just add 0 to the number you are multiplying it by.

$$8 \times 10 = 80$$

or

$$6 \times 10 = 60$$

16 5 times table

Whiffy's very sad about P's "surprise". He had expected something more fun, like this trick for remembering your 5 times table.

When you multiply 5 by an odd number, the answer will end in 5.

$$7 \times 5 = 35$$

When you multiply 5 by an even number, the answer will end in 0.

$$4 \times 5 = 20$$

Here is a number line of Whiffy's sad tears to help you.

0 5 10 15 20 25 30 35 40 45 50

If you can imagine how noisy P's scream is, you should be able to write in the answers to these sums.

1 10 × 2 = ____

2 10 × 4 = ____

3 7 × ____ = 70

4 ____ × 10 = 50

5 ____ × 10 = 80

6 6 × 10 = ____

7 ____ × 10 = 10

8 9 × 10 = ____

9 4 × 10 = ____

10 10 × 10 = ____

For each sum, write down whether 5 is being multiplied by an odd or even number. Then fill in the answers.

1 5 odd ×5 = ____

2 2 ____ ×5 = ____

3 10 ____ ×5 = ____

4 1 ____ ×5 = ____

5 3 ____ ×5 = ____

6 9 ____ ×5 = ____

7 7 ____ ×5 = ____

8 6 ____ ×5 = ____

9 8 ____ ×5 = ____

10 4 ____ ×5 = ____

Waldo tried chasing his tail. Again, everyone smiled, but they didn't laugh. Ezzo did some somersaults, then hopped on one leg. "Sorry. It's just not very funny," sighed Christabell.

Whiffy went to find his bird costume. He came back with some of the feathers. "Tickling makes everyone laugh," he said, and he used the feathers to tickle Christabell and Ezzo.

"Oh, stop it, Whiffy! Ha, ha, ha!" Christabell and Ezzo shrieked. They giggled so much it was hard to stop.

No clown costume is complete without a bow tie! Add one to your list at the front of the book.

17 Sharing 2 and 3

Christabell shared out some things she had bought for the party amongst her friends.

She had 8 party poppers, which she shared between Waldo and Whiffy.

8 shared between 2 gives 4 each.

She also had 6 party hats, which she shared between Ezzo, Waldo and Whiffy.

6 shared between 3 gives 2 each.

18 Sharing 4 and 5

All 4 monster friends shared their best ideas for trying to make P laugh. Ezzo likes jokes and has 16 joke books. If he shared these books between himself and his 3 friends, how many books would each monster get?

16 shared between 4 gives 4 each.

If Ezzo only had 15 books to share between 5 people, how many books would each monster get?

15 shared between 5 gives 3 each.

Share out all these lovely things for the ball between the monster friends, and write down how many each monster gets.

1  6 between 2 gives ☐ each.

2  10 between 2 gives ☐ each.

3  9 between 3 gives ☐ each.

4  3 between 3 gives ☐ each.

5 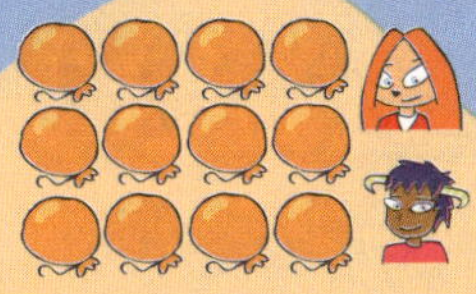 12 between 2 gives ☐ each.

6  15 between 3 gives ☐ each.

7 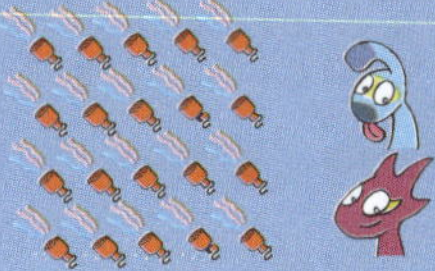 20 between 2 gives ☐ each.

8  12 between 3 gives ☐ each.

9  16 between 2 gives ☐ each.

10 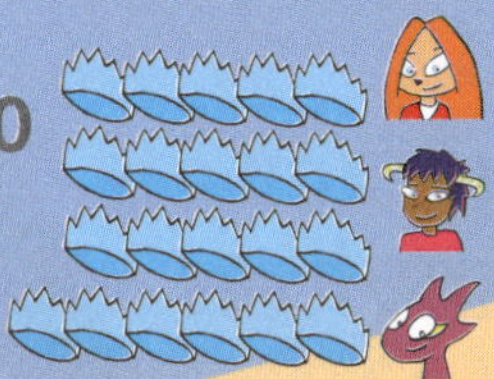 21 between 3 gives ☐ each.

Share Ezzo's joke books between him and his friends. Write down how many each friend gets.

1  8 between 4 gives ☐ each.

2  10 between 5 gives ☐ each.

3  12 between 4 gives ☐ each.

4  16 between 4 gives ☐ each.

5  15 between 5 gives ☐ each.

6  16 between 4 gives ☐ each.

7  5 between 5 gives ☐ each.

8  20 between 4 gives ☐ each.

9  24 between 4 gives ☐ each.

10  20 between 5 gives ☐ each.

"That's the answer!" Whiffy declared. "We will tickle P and save Monster City. And if I run out of feathers on my costume, there are still loads left in my pillow."

Later that day, monsters from all over town arrived at the palace for the ball. They each wore a fancy dress costume in lots of bright colours.

Everyone was very excited and pleased to be invited to such a posh party.

You want to arrive at the ball in style! How about a fabulous monster limousine to take all your party goodies?

19 Dividing by 2 and 3

Whiffy divided up the feathers from his costume to make into tickling sticks. Dividing is just like sharing.

6 feathers shared between 2 tickling sticks gives 3 feathers on each stick.

$6 \div 2 = 3$

12 feathers shared between 3 tickling sticks give 4 feathers on each.

$12 \div 3 = 4$

20 Dividing by 4 and 5

Whiffy divided the feathers left in the pillow between his friends, so they could make each other giggle whenever they felt like it!

If there were 16 feathers left and he divided them between himself, Ezzo, Christabell and Waldo, how many would they have each? 16 shared between 4 gives 4 each.

$$16 \div 4 = 4$$

If there are 10 feathers left and Whiffy divided them between 5 friendly monsters at the ball, how many would they have each? 10 shared between 5 gives 2 each.

$$10 \div 5 = 2$$

Write down how many feathers there would be on each tickling stick.

1 8 shared between 2 gives feathers on each. $8 \div 2 =$

2 9 shared between 3 gives feathers on each. $9 \div 3 =$

3 6 shared between 3 gives feathers on each. $6 \div 3 =$

4 12 shared between 2 gives feathers on each. $12 \div 2 =$

5 12 shared between 3 gives feathers on each. $12 \div 3 =$

6 16 shared between 2 gives feathers on each. $16 \div 2 =$

7 18 shared between 3 gives feathers on each. $18 \div 3 =$

8 15 shared between 3 gives feathers on each. $15 \div 3 =$

9 14 shared between 2 gives feathers on each. $14 \div 2 =$

10 21 shared between 3 gives feathers on each. $21 \div 3 =$

Divide the number of feathers between the monsters and write down the answers.

1 15 shared between 5 monsters gives feathers each. $15 \div 5 =$

2 8 shared between 4 monsters gives feathers each. $8 \div 4 =$

3 35 shared between 5 monsters gives feathers each. $35 \div 5 =$

4 20 shared between 4 monsters gives feathers each. $20 \div 4 =$

5 12 shared between 4 monsters gives feathers each. $12 \div 4 =$

6 20 shared between 5 monsters gives feathers each. $20 \div 5 =$

7 50 shared between 5 monsters gives feathers each. $50 \div 5 =$

8 24 shared between 4 monsters gives feathers each. $24 \div 4 =$

9 40 shared between 4 monsters gives feathers each. $40 \div 4 =$

10 25 shared between 5 monsters gives feathers each. $25 \div 5 =$

The bad monsters wore their best fancy dress costumes, too. P was dressed like a queen with a sparkling crown on her head. Edgar was dressed like a spaceman. Flob (who wasn't quite as bad as the others) was dressed like a big, fat black and yellow bee.

There was music and dancing, balloons, poppers and party hats. It seemed like a wonderful party. "Don't be fooled," Ezzo whispered to Whiffy. "The bad monsters are just pretending to be friendly."

Music, dancing and balloons! What a wonderful party! Remember to put on your party hat.

21 Multiplying and dividing

All the monsters at the ball have something in common. They are all wearing fancy dress. Multiplying and dividing numbers have something in common, too!

Here are 2 lots of 6 fancy dress masks.

2 lots of 6 makes 12.

$2 \times 6 = 12$

12 divided by 2 makes 6.

$12 \div 2 = 6$

22 Number trios

Trio means 3. The trio of bad monsters – P, Edgar and Flob – all have something in common. They are nasty, horrible and evil. Well, Flob isn't always evil, but he's not very good either!

How many times can we use this trio of numbers in different types of problems?

$4 \times 6 = 24$ $6 \times 4 = 24$

$24 \div 6 = 4$ $24 \div 4 = 6$

Read the sums out loud. Then write in all the missing numbers.

1 2 lots of 5 makes 10.
$2 \times 5 =$ ____
10 divided by 2 makes 5.
$10 \div 2 =$ ____

2 3 lots of 5 makes 15.
$3 \times 5 =$ ____
15 divided by 3 makes 5.
$15 \div 3 =$ ____

3 5 lots of 5 makes 25.
$5 \times 5 =$ ____
25 divided by 5 makes 5.
$25 \div 5 =$ ____

4 4 lots of 6 makes 24.
$4 \times 6 =$ ____
24 divided by 4 makes 6.
$24 \div 4 =$ ____

5 2 lots of 10 makes ____.
$2 \times 10 =$ ____
20 divided by 2 makes ____.
$20 \div 2 =$ ____

6 5 lots of 4 makes ____.
$5 \times 4 =$ ____
20 divided by 5 makes ____.
$20 \div 5 =$ ____

7 3 lots of 7 makes ____.
$3 \times 7 =$ ____
21 divided by 3 makes ____.
$21 \div 3 =$ ____

8 4 lots of 8 makes ____.
$4 \times 8 =$ ____
32 divided by 4 makes ____.
$32 \div 4 =$ ____

9 5 lots of 9 makes ____.
$5 \times 9 =$ ____
45 divided by 5 makes ____.
$45 \div 5 =$ ____

10 3 lots of 7 makes ____.
$3 \times 7 =$ ____
21 divided by 3 makes ____.
$21 \div 3 =$ ____

Write out as many questions as possible from the trio of numbers and fill in the answers, too.

1 18 3 6
3 × ____ = ____
2 × ____ = ____
18 ÷ ____ = ____
____ ÷ 2 = ____

2 4 3 12
____ × 3 = ____
4 × ____ = ____
12 ÷ ____ = ____
____ ÷ 3 = ____

3 5 15 3
____ × 3 = ____
____ × 5 = ____
____ ÷ 5 = ____
15 ÷ ____ = ____

4 2 16 8
____ × ____ = ____
____ × ____ = ____
____ ÷ ____ = ____
____ ÷ ____ = ____

5 21 7 3
____ × ____ = ____
____ × ____ = ____
____ ÷ ____ = ____
____ ÷ ____ = ____

6 2 10 20
____ × ____ = ____
____ × ____ = ____
____ ÷ ____ = ____
____ ÷ ____ = ____

7 18 3 6
____ × ____ = ____
____ × ____ = ____
____ ÷ ____ = ____
____ ÷ ____ = ____

8 9 27 3
____ × ____ = ____
____ × ____ = ____
____ ÷ ____ = ____
____ ÷ ____ = ____

9 24 4 6
____ × ____ = ____
____ × ____ = ____
____ ÷ ____ = ____
____ ÷ ____ = ____

At last, P stood up to make a speech. "Welcome everybody. I am glad you came to my ball," she began. All the guests clapped their hands.

"And now for the big surprise ..." Then she opened her mouth to scream. Suddenly, Ezzo leapt through the air with a karate kick and knocked P over. Then Waldo sat on her, while Whiffy used the feathers from his bird costume to tickle her. "Hey!" yelled Edgar as he rushed towards Whiffy, but Christabell tripped him up!

Ezzo is very strong! You had better pour him some fizzy pop. He is going to be thirsty after that karate kick!

23 Multiplying

Before P made her speech, more and more monsters were arriving at the ball. They were multiplying by the minute!

Hope you have a ball solving these multiplying problems!

24 Dividing

As P stood up to make her speech, she saw the monsters had divided into different groups. Some were dancing, others were eating and some were chatting to their friends.

Here are some dividing problems for you to answer. You may get a big surprise when you have finished!

See if you can write down the answers to all these multiplying sums.

1 $6 \times 5 =$ ____ and $5 \times 6 =$ ____

2 $4 \times 10 =$ ____ and $10 \times 4 =$ ____

3 $8 \times 3 =$ ____ and $3 \times 8 =$ ____

4 $2 \times 9 =$ ____ and $9 \times 2 =$ ____

5 $5 \times 8 =$ ____ and $8 \times 5 =$ ____

6 $7 \times 4 =$ ____ and $4 \times 7 =$ ____

7 $3 \times 9 =$ ____ and $9 \times 3 =$ ____

8 $7 \times 3 =$ ____ and $3 \times 7 =$ ____

9 $8 \times 2 =$ ____ and $2 \times 8 =$ ____

10 $4 \times 5 =$ ____ and $5 \times 4 =$ ____

See how quickly you can fill in all the spaces for these dividing sums.

1 $20 \div 5 =$ ____ and $20 \div$ ____ $= 5$

2 $24 \div 4 =$ ____ and $24 \div$ ____ $= 4$

3 $30 \div 3 =$ ____ and $30 \div$ ____ $= 3$

4 $12 \div 3 =$ ____ and $12 \div$ ____ $= 3$

5 $18 \div 6 =$ ____ and $18 \div$ ____ $= 6$

6 $9 \div 3 =$ ____ and $9 \div$ ____ $= 3$

7 $45 \div 5 =$ ____ and $45 \div$ ____ $= 5$

8 $21 \div 7 =$ ____ and $21 \div$ ____ $= 7$

9 $36 \div 4 =$ ____ and $36 \div$ ____ $= 4$

10 $16 \div 2 =$ ____ and $16 \div$ ____ $= 2$

Whiffy knew all the best places for tickling. First he tickled the back of P's knees. Then he tickled the insides of her elbows and underneath her chin.

"Ha, ha, ha!" she giggled, unable to stop.

"Ha, ha, ha! Stop it!" She began to shriek with laughter.

"Ho, ho, ho!" She laughed louder than ever and snorted in between the laughs.

Everyone else at the party began to giggle, too.

25 Pictograms

Different parts of P's body were tickled with a different number of feathers. We can show this information on a pictogram – 3 feathers were used to tickle the back of her knees, 2 for her elbows and 5 for under her chin, where she was very ticklish indeed!

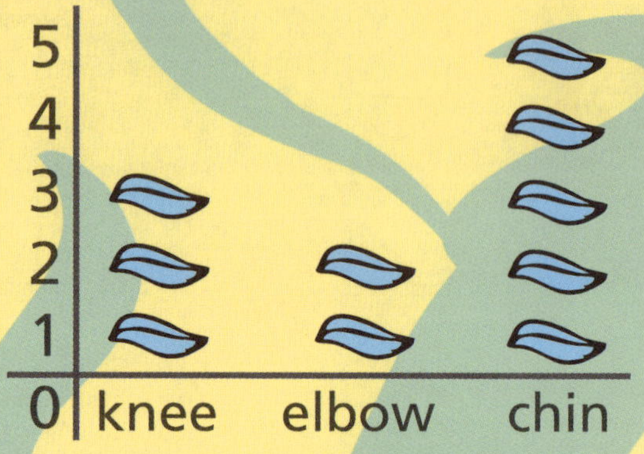

26 Graphs

Another way of showing information is on a graph. Here's one that shows how loudly or quietly P laughed when she was tickled on the different parts of her body.

Good job Waldo is sitting on P! Take your monster pet to the ball too.

Using this pictogram, try to answer the questions about P being tickled.

1 How many feathers were used to tickle P's elbows?

2 What was the largest number of feathers used to tickle a part of P's body?

3 Is the number of feathers used to tickle P's knees larger or smaller than used for her chin? ____________

4 How many more feathers are used to tickle P's chin than her elbows?

5 How many feathers are used to tickle P's chin?

6 How many feathers were used altogether to tickle P's elbows and knees?

7 Which part of P's body was tickled with smallest number of feathers? ____________

8 Is the number of feathers used to tickle P's elbows larger or smaller than used for her knees? ____________

9 What was the smallest number of feathers used to tickle a part of P's body?

10 How many feathers were used altogether to tickle P?

Look at the graph, then write down the answers to these questions.

1 Which body part was being tickled when P laughed quietly? ____________

2 Did she laugh more loudly when she was tickled on her knees or her chin? ____________

3 How did she laugh when she was tickled on her knees? ____________

4 Where would you tickle P if you wanted to make her laugh extremely loudly? ____________

5 Are there any body parts where P was tickled and she laughed more quietly still? ____________

6 Did she laugh more quietly when she was tickled on her chin or her elbows? ____________

7 Where would you tickle P if you wanted to make her laugh quietly? ____________

8 Which body part was being tickled when P laughed loudest? ____________

9 How did she laugh when she was tickled on her chin? ____________

10 Was P ever silent when she was tickled? ____________

Even Flob grinned. And Edgar's mouth turned up at the corners and twitched, which was almost a smile. He just couldn't help it. P turned bright red and ran away to hide.

"Go home, you horrible lot," Edgar shouted at the guests. "The party is over."

"No it's not," they shouted back. "We want to dance and eat more cake."

They ignored Edgar and carried on having a good time.

There is a lot more food to eat! Time to hand around some yummy sandwiches!

27 O'clock and half past

There are two big clocks in the ballroom, so the monsters can tell the time.

The clocks show it is 6 o'clock.

And now they show it is half past six.

28 Quarter to and quarter past

The two ballroom clocks keep ticking away.

The clocks show quarter past seven.

A bit later they show quarter to eight.

Draw the hands or write the numbers on the clock, so the two clocks show the same time.

1 

2 

3 

4 

5 

6 

7 

8 

9 

10 

Fill in the missing numbers or hands on these clocks with the right time.

1 Quarter past eight

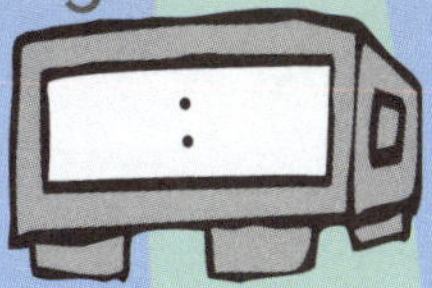

2 Quarter to ten

3 Quarter to eight

4 Quarter past three

5 Quarter to nine

6 Quarter past two

7 Quarter past nine

8 Quarter to five

9 Quarter past six

10 Quarter to eleven

Edgar ran away and hid with P, but Flob stayed at the ball. He was having such fun. He loved wearing his bee costume, and danced round and round singing, "Buzz, buzz!"

"I had a wonderful time," Whiffy sighed happily when the ball was over. "The tickling was the best fun of all." Then he danced with Christabell, Ezzo and Waldo all the way home to Smile Street!

Even Flob loves to dance. Play a tune on your harmonica so everyone can dance all the way home!

29 Pounds and pence

Imagine you have a bag of all the different pound and pence coins.

If you wanted to buy each part of Flob's colourful bee costume, which coins would you need?

£2 + 50p + 5p = £2.55

20p + 2p = 22p

10p + 5p + 1p = 16p

£1 + 2p + 1p = £1.03

30 Fractions

As it got later, the monsters started to go home to their beds. The younger monsters left first, so there was only half the number of monsters at the ball. Then half more left and there was only quarter of the monsters left. Half and quarter are called fractions. They are written in numbers like this:

$\frac{1}{2}$ (half) $\frac{1}{4}$ (quarter)

$\frac{1}{2}$ of 8 monsters = 4 monsters

$\frac{1}{4}$ of 4 monsters = 1 monster

How much would it cost to buy these fancy dress items? Write in the missing amounts.

1 a crown

50p + 2p =

2 a space helmet

£2 + 1p =

3 a pirate sword

10p + 5p =

4 a silver mask

50p + 5p =

5 Waldo's flower collar

20p + 1p =

6 a stripy bee t-shirt

 + 50p + = £2.55

7 a chef's apron

 + 20p = 40p

8 a paper beak

5p + = 7p

9 a cape

£1 + 50p =

10 fairy wings

20p + 5p =

Do these sums, then write down the fraction of monsters left.

1 $\frac{1}{2}$ of 4 monsters = ☐

2 $\frac{1}{4}$ of 8 monsters = ☐

3 $\frac{1}{2}$ of 14 monsters = ☐

4 $\frac{1}{2}$ of 12 monsters = ☐

5 $\frac{1}{4}$ of 16 monsters = ☐

6 $\frac{1}{4}$ of 20 monsters = ☐

7 $\frac{1}{2}$ of 18 monsters = ☐

8 $\frac{1}{4}$ of 12 monsters = ☐

9 $\frac{1}{4}$ of 4 monsters = ☐

10 $\frac{1}{2}$ of 20 monsters = ☐

Answers

Test 1 Counting to 100

1 10 11 12 13 14 15 16 17 18 19
2 80 81 82 83 84 85 86 87 88 89
3 40 41 42 43 44 45 46 47 48 49
4 71 72 73 74 75 76 77 78 79 80
5 34 35 36 37 38 39 40 41 42 43
6 85 86 87 88 89 90 91 92 93 94
7 47 48 49 50 51 52 53 54 55 56
8 69 70 71 72 73 74 75 76 77 78
9 91 92 93 94 95 96 97 98 99 100
10 53 54 55 56 57 58 59 60 61 62

Test 2 Tens and units

1 10 + 8 = 18
2 20 + 4 = 24
3 50 + 9 = 59
4 90 + 8 = 98
5 60 + 5 = 65
6 70 + 3 = 73
7 80 + 2 = 82
8 30 + 4 = 34
9 40 + 6 = 46
10 50 + 4 = 54

Test 3 Adding sets

1 6 + 4 = 10
2 3 + 6 = 9
3 5 + 7 = 12
4 2 + 9 = 11
5 7 + 7 = 14
6 8 + 9 = 17
7 11 + 4 = 15
8 6 + 12 = 18
9 4 + 15 = 19
10 9 + 12 = 21

Test 4 Taking away sets

1 12 – 3 = 9
2 7 – 6 = 1
3 10 – 7 = 3
4 9 – 1 = 8
5 15 – 8 = 7
6 11 – 6 = 5
7 13 – 9 = 4
8 14 – 5 = 9
9 16 – 11 = 5
10 14 – 7 = 7

Test 5 Missing numbers

1 10 + 4 = 14, 14 – 10 = 4
2 9 + 5 = 14, 14 – 9 = 5
3 16 + 2 = 18, 18 – 16 = 2
4 12 + 7 = 19, 19 – 12 = 7
5 5 + 12 = 17, 17 – 5 = 12
6 7 + 15 = 22, 22 – 15 = 7
7 9 + 8 = 17, 17 – 8 = 9
8 17 + 5 = 22, 22 – 17 = 5
9 20 + 11 = 31, 31 – 20 = 11
10 14 + 15 = 29, 29 – 15 = 14

Test 6 Adding and taking away tens

1 3 + 5 = 8, 30 + 50 = 80
2 6 + 4 = 10, 60 + 40 = 100
3 3 + 3 = 6, 30 + 30 = 60
4 4 + 2 = 6, 40 + 20 = 60
5 6 + 7 = 13, 60 + 70 = 130
6 2 + 9 = 11, 20 + 90 = 110
7 8 + 5 = 13, 80 + 50 = 130
8 7 + 10 = 17, 70 + 100 = 170
9 12 + 4 = 16, 120 + 40 = 160
10 16 + 9 = 25, 160 + 90 = 250

Test 7 Adding money

1 5p + 12p = 17p
2 22p + 7p = 29p
3 50p + 16p = 66p
4 11p + 23p = 34p
5 61p + 9p = 70p
6 72p + 20p = 92p
7 16p + 43p = 59p
8 24p + 61p = 85p
9 8p + 88p = 96p
10 43p + 46p = 89p

Test 8 Taking away money

1 40p – 20p = 20p
2 75p – 25p = 50p
3 20p – 16p = 4p
4 95p – 55p = 40p
5 24p – 12p = 12p
6 68p – 48p = 20p
7 73p – 41p = 32p
8 49p – 37p = 12p
9 96p – 59p = 37p
10 £1.00 – 42p = 58p

Test 9 Shapes

1 triangle, 3
2 square, 4
3 circle, 0
4 octagon, 8
5 triangle, 3
6 pentagon, 5
7 oval, 0
8 rectangle, 4
9 hexagon, 6
10 quadrilateral/ rectangle, 4

Test 10 Measuring

1 a drawing of a 2cm high cake
2 a drawing of a 5cm high cake
3 a drawing of a 1cm high cake
4 a drawing of a 4cm high cake
5 No
6 Yes
7 No
8 Yes
9 Yes
10 No

Test 11 Groups of 2 and 3

1 2 + 2 + 2 = 6
2 3 + 3 + 3 + 3 = 12
3 2 + 2 + 2 + 2 + 2 = 10
4 3 + 3 + 3 = 9
5 3 + 3 + 3 + 3 + 3 + 3 = 18
6 2 + 2 + 2 + 2 + 2 + 2 + 2 + 2 = 16
7 2 + 2 + 2 + 2 + 2 + 2 = 12
8 2 + 2 = 4
9 3 + 3 + 3 + 3 + 3 + 3 + 3 = 21
10 3 + 3 + 3 + 3 + 3 = 15

Test 12 Groups of 4 and 5

1 4 + 4 + 4 + 4 + 4 + 4 = 24
2 5 + 5 + 5 = 15
3 4 + 4 + 4 + 4 = 16
4 4 + 4 + 4 + 4 + 4 + 4 + 4 = 28
5 5 + 5 + 5 + 5 + 5 = 25
6 5 + 5 + 5 + 5 + 5 + 5 + 5 + 5 = 40
7 4 + 4 + 4 + 4 + 4 + 4 = 24
8 5 + 5 + 5 + 5 = 20
9 4 + 4 + 4 + 4 + 4 = 20
10 5 + 5 + 5 + 5 + 5 + 5 + 5 + 5 + 5 = 45

Test 13 2 times table

1 3 × 2 = 6
2 7 × 2 = 14
3 6 × 2 = 12
4 2 × 2 = 4
5 10 × 2 = 20
6 8 × 2 = 16
7 5 × 2 = 10
8 7 × 2 = 14
9 4 × 2 = 8
10 9 × 2 = 18

Test 14 3 times table

1 3 × 3 = 9
2 6 × 3 = 18
3 7 × 3 = 21
4 9 × 3 = 27
5 5 × 3 = 15
6 8 × 3 = 24
7 4 × 3 = 12
8 2 × 3 = 6
9 10 × 3 = 30
10 7 × 3 = 21